An illustrated souvenir

BROWNSEA ISLAND

Dorset

The National Trust

The entrance building for visitors to Brownsea

Introduction

'I had no idea I had such a delightful spot in my kingdom,' exclaimed the Prince Regent after a trip to Brownsea in 1818. Today this 500-acre island of pinewood, heathland and salt-marsh still has plenty to surprise and delight the thousands who visit it each summer.

Over the centuries Brownsea has had a remarkably varied history as military stronghold, industrial site, wildlife refuge and place of recreation and adventure. It has been pillaged by Viking raiders and blitzed by Nazi bombers. In the nineteenth century Brownsea was extensively mined for china clay. Work in the pottery brought in Brownsea settlers, who formed a close island community with its own school and brass band. Brownsea is still looked after by local people, but now for the benefit of all.

As the south coast has been increasingly developed, the island has become an even more important sanctuary for wildlife, especially red squirrels and wading birds. It is also a place that has always welcomed human beings seeking sanctuary. In 1907 Baden-Powell held the first Scout camp on the island; today Brownsea still seems a world away from the bustle of Poole across the harbour.

View from the visitors' quay towards Brownsea Castle (private)

The muddy shoreline on the south-east corner of the island

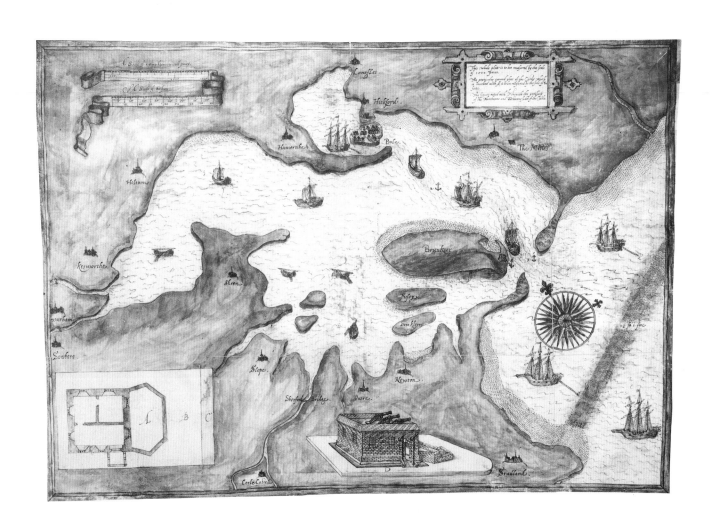

Tudor fortress

There has been a settled community on Brownsea since at least 500BC, which has left behind shiny black pottery made from the local clay. By the ninth century AD the monks of Cerne Abbey near Dorchester had built a little chapel on the island, which was destroyed by Viking invaders under King Cnut (Canute) in 1015.

Following the Dissolution of the Monasteries in the 1530s, control of Brownsea passed from Cerne Abbey to Henry VIII. The King recognised the strategic importance of the island, guarding the approaches to the thriving port of Poole, and encouraged the local merchants to build a stone blockhouse on the south-east corner of the island in 1545–7 – the first Brownsea Castle. It became one of a string of similar forts designed to defend the south coast against invasion from the Continent.

The castle's defences were almost put to the test 40 years later, when the Spanish Armada engaged the English fleet between Portland Bill and the Isle of Wight on 2–3 August 1588. Fortunately, the Spanish fleet was beaten off.

Sir Christopher Hatton, who was granted Brownsea Castle by Queen Elizabeth in 1576 (National Portrait Gallery). His officials in the castle were often at loggerheads with the Poole merchants over ships seeking safe passage into Poole harbour

The engagement of the English and Spanish fleets between Portland Bill and the Isle of Wight (2–3 August 1588). Engraving by John Pine, 1739 (National Maritime Museum)

This map of 1597 shows the strategic importance of Brownsea Island guarding the entrance to Poole harbour (British Library). It also illustrates the single-storey blockhouse put up in 1545–7, which was defended on three sides by a moat and on the fourth by three cannons on the roof

5

The seventeenth and eighteenth centuries

From the 1650s Brownsea was owned by a succession of MPs, who transformed the appearance of the island. The first was Sir Robert Clayton, a City of London merchant of immense wealth who acquired Brownsea during the Commonwealth and was one of the leading Protestant opponents of Charles II. His heirs sold the island around 1726 to William Benson.

Benson, an amateur architect who ousted the aged Christopher Wren as Surveyor-General of the King's Works, decided to convert Brownsea Castle into a residence, to the alarm of the Poole merchants, who wanted to retain it as a fortress. Benson was also a knowledgeable botanist who planted many trees on the island, the rotting stumps of which offer attractive homes for insects. He seems to have dabbled in black magic and lost his sanity towards the end of his life.

Sir Humphrey Sturt, an influential local landowner and MP, inherited Brownsea in 1765 and set about rebuilding Benson's castle on the grand scale. He is said to have spent over £50,000 just on the adjoining ornamental gardens. One of the new breed of agricultural 'improvers', Sturt shipped in bargeloads of manure and soap ash to improve the light, sandy soil and introduced crop rotation to the island. His son Charles was often away fighting in the Napoleonic Wars and his grandson Henry preferred the family's grander Dorset seat, Crichel House, where he entertained the Prince Regent in 1818.

Sir Robert Clayton, MP (1629–1707) owned Brownsea for over 50 years. His grandiose tomb, by Richard Crutcher in Bletchingley church, Surrey, shows him wearing his chain of office as Lord Mayor of London

Sir Humphrey Sturt, MP (?1725–86) greatly enlarged the castle, adding a four-storey tower with lower wings on three sides and Palladian windows. He also laid out a walled courtyard with corner pavilions and decorative battlements on the site of the present walled garden. Engraving from John Hutchins's *History of Dorset* (1773)

View from the south coast of the island over Poole harbour towards Corfe Castle

Industry comes to Brownsea

In 1852 Brownsea was again up for sale. While an ex-Indian Army officer, Col William Waugh, was looking over the island, his wife Mary noticed a white mud sticking to the end of her walking-stick which she believed to be china clay. A geologist confirmed her suspicions, and the excited couple, seeing a chance to make their fortune, bought the island for £13,000. Waugh erected a huge pottery works at the north-west end of the island, together with a village to house the factory workers, which he named Maryland after his wife. At its height Branksey Clay & Pottery Company employed over 200 people, many of whom rowed over from Studland to the island every day.

Alas, the Brownsea clay proved unsuitable for making fine china, but Waugh continued to pour money into the project with increasing desperation. Disaster finally struck when a group of local businessmen arrived to ask Col Waugh to stand for parliament. Mary Waugh was rather deaf and, thinking that they had come about unpaid bills, pleaded for more time to settle. When the tradesmen compared notes, the Waughs' ambitious enterprise collapsed like a pack of cards, and they were forced to flee to Spain.

Between 1852 and 1857 William Waugh added a new south-east front in the Tudor style to Brownsea Castle, and also built the gatehouse (*above*) and the family pier with its castellated watch-towers (*left*)

Contemporary engraving of the Waughs' pottery factory. Stacked outside are the drainage pipes which were all that could be made from the coarse Brownsea clay

The neo-Gothic church of St Mary the Virgin, also built by Waugh, was consecrated in October 1854

Renaissance and ruin

After lengthy legal argument among the Waughs' creditors, Brownsea was finally sold in 1873 to the Hon. George Cavendish-Bentinck. He kept the pottery works going until 1887, but concentrated on improving agriculture on the island, bringing in pedigree Guernsey and Jersey cows, and planting maize, barley, and spring and winter oats.

Cavendish-Bentinck inherited his family's passion for art collecting. He filled Brownsea Castle with a spectacular array of Italian Renaissance sculpture, some of which can still be seen decorating the church and the quay buildings. When he died in 1891, the island was bought by Major Kenneth Balfour; only five years later the castle caught fire. There was no fire-engine on Brownsea and, despite the human bucket chain formed by the islanders, the building was gutted. Undaunted, Balfour rebuilt the castle complete with modern fire hydrants, but in 1901 put it on the market.

The well-head in St Mary's churchyard marks the Cavendish-Bentinck family tomb

In 1896 Brownsea Castle was almost completely destroyed by fire

The carved Renaissance relief of St Christopher was brought to Brownsea by George Cavendish-Bentinck and set into the wall of the quay

Edwardian grandeur

With the coming of Charles and Florence van Raalte in 1901, Brownsea entered a period of unparalleled prosperity and grandeur. The castle was filled with the Van Raaltes' splendid collection of musical instruments, which included an electric piano that turned out Gilbert and Sullivan ditties. The family's steam launch, the *Blunderbuss*, brought over Queen Marie of Romania and numerous other wealthy guests to the elegant summer house-parties the Van Raaltes held on the island. They could play golf on the course that had been built to the west of the castle, or shoot game in the woods.

One of the more unusual visitors was Guglielmo Marconi, who for many years conducted his experiments with wireless telegraphy at the Haven Hotel opposite Brownsea. He was a particular favourite of the Van Raaltes' children, Margot and Babs, to whom he gave a wireless set: 'We "Morsed" messages to each other and got so keen on the Morse code, that we could "left eye right eye" across the luncheon table!' Brownsea was a paradise for the young Van Raaltes, who ran wild in the woods, sailed in the harbour and often swam the mile and a quarter to the mainland.

Charles van Raalte died in 1908 and was buried beneath a white marble tomb in Brownsea church. His wife continued to keep up Brownsea to the same high standards for another seventeen years, until, in 1925, she finally decided to sell up.

(*Above*) Florence van Raalte

(*Below*) Charles van Raalte

The sundial in the formal Italian Garden laid out by the Van Raaltes in the grounds of Brownsea Castle

The south front of Brownsea Castle from the sea

The first Scout camp

In the 1860s the Admiralty had been considering buying Brownsea to replace Dartmouth as a base for training naval cadets. So it was appropriate that, at Charles van Raalte's invitation, Robert Baden-Powell, the hero of Mafeking, should have chosen the island for his first Scout camp. He chose 22 boys to join him, some the public-school children of his acquaintances, others working-class lads from the Poole and Bournemouth Boys' Brigades.

In August 1907 they set up their tents on the south coast of the island. The day began at dawn with the blast of an African kudu horn. After a glass of milk and a biscuit, followed by 30 minutes' physical training and prayers, the boys broke up into separate patrols – the Wolves, Bulls, Curlews and Ravens – for stalking and tracking, building shelters, putting up tents and mock whale-hunts in boats. In the evening there were brief talks on Scouting techniques, and then Baden-Powell told yarns of life on the African veld round the camp-fire. The success of this first camp encouraged Baden-Powell to publish his *Scouting for Boys* the following year, and from this modest beginning the international Scouting movement grew rapidly.

Major-General Robert Baden-Powell wearing the prototype Scout uniform. Margot van Raalte described him as 'a little man with large freckles, a bony nose and thin hair. He had a sandy-coloured moustache, and twinkling blue eyes'

Learning how to stuff a fern mattress

The monument to the first Scout camp, held on Brownsea in August 1907. There have been peacocks on the island since the Van Raaltes' time

Life on Brownsea

Many of those who had been drawn to Brownsea in the early 1850s by the prospect of work at the pottery factory, stayed on after it closed and over the following 50 years formed a small but close community. Under the estate manager Tresco Brown, who rode round the island on his boneshaker bicycle, they worked in the fields, digging peat, growing daffodils for Covent Garden, or ploughing the small area of arable land. Many islanders were employed in the castle, either as house staff or looking after the Van Raaltes' immaculate garden. When there were shooting parties, they dressed in 'hunting green' and served as beaters.

The two boatmen were a vital part of island life: Tom Dean, who came from one of the oldest families on Brownsea and who skippered the Van Raaltes' *Blunderbuss*, decked out in naval jacket with shiny buttons; and Tom Biggs, 'with the sea in his blue eyes and a golden beard'. Many estate workers played in the island band; indeed they were asked before they were taken on whether they could play an instrument. The island's school, next to the clock tower, was run by the fearsome Miss Fookes; her successor, Miss Dunn, was rather more easy-going.

Those who were brought up on Brownsea in the early years of this century remember it as an idyllic time, but the idyll was to be short-lived. Of the 30 Brownsea islanders who went away to the Great War in 1914, only six returned. And in 1927 their entire way of life was to be turned upside-down.

The daffodils were shipped over to Poole in boxes made by the islanders during the winter, and then sent by train to London

Daffodil-growing became a major part of the island's economy in the years after Charles van Raalte's death in 1908

A tea-party for the islanders at Brownsea Castle, around 1901–6

Return to nature

In November 1927 Mrs Mary Bonham-Christie bought the island for £125,000 and moved into what had been the agent's house on the quay. Opposed to blood sports and indeed to the exploitation of animals by man in any form, she banned fishing and allowed the farm animals to roam wild. The farm, dairy, orchards and daffodil fields were abandoned, and the island gradually reverted to natural heathland.

For the majority of the redundant estate workers this meant a sad exodus to the mainland, but for the local wildlife it was a godsend. While their habitat shrank with the rapid urbanisation of the south coast, Brownsea remained as an increasingly important sanctuary. However, even that was threatened in 1934, when the island was ravaged by a fire which burnt out of control for a week.

In May 1940 Brownsea provided a brief haven for exhausted Dutch and Belgian refugees, who had taken to small boats to escape the Nazi invasion of the Low Countries and had been shepherded along the south coast into Poole harbour by the Royal Navy. Flares were also lit on the western end of the island to mislead German bombers seeking out harbour installations in Poole and Bournemouth. As a result the estate cottages at Maryland, which had mostly been lying empty since 1927, were further damaged.

Mrs Mary Bonham-Christie, who bought Brownsea in 1927

The great Brownsea fire, 18 July 1934

All that remains of the village of Maryland, which was largely abandoned after Mrs Bonham-Christie took over

The National Trust takes over

The interior of the church today

In April 1961 Mrs Bonham-Christie died at the age of 96, and her grandson was obliged to put the island on the market to meet death duties. When rumours of plans for a marina or luxury housing on Brownsea began to circulate, the Brownsea Island Appeal Committee was formed by a group of concerned local people, with Leslie Millier as Chairman and Helen Brotherton as Honorary Secretary; its aim was to protect the island in its unspoilt state. After the Treasury had accepted the island in lieu of death duties, the National Trust agreed to take over responsibility for it, provided that an endowment of £100,000 was raised. A nationwide campaign was launched to save the island, and sums large and small came in from local businesses and individuals, charitable trusts and Scouts organisations. The John Lewis Partnership was a particularly generous donor, which also repaired Brownsea Castle and rented it from the Trust as a hotel for its employees. By May 1962 the money had been raised and Brownsea was safe.

Through the great winter of 1962–3 the new Head Warden, Alan Bromby, and his assistant, Jack Battrick, worked with numerous volunteers to prepare the island for visitors. Tracks were cleared through the rampant rhododendrons and firebreaks cut to prevent a repetition of the disastrous fire of 1934. On 15 May 1963 Jack Battrick wrote in this diary, 'A sultry, but brilliant summer's day found us celebrating our grand overture.' Among the audience at the formal opening ceremony were two of those who had taken part in the first Scout camp 55 years before.

The churchyard of St Mary's in the overgrown state in which it came to the National Trust

Landscape

Brownsea's 500 acres support an extraordinarily wide range of habitats – from muddy seashore to brackish lagoon and freshwater lake, from open grassland and heath to pinewoods and broadleafed woodland. Most are the work of man. Until the sixteenth century the island seems to have been largely open heath. Succeeding generations of Brownsea's owners planted extensive tracts of pine, sycamore, poplar and chestnut, drained St Andrew's Bay to create new pasture, and enclosed fields for growing daffodils. This rich mixture survived the 1934 fire and the benign neglect of Mrs Bonham-Christie, and during the last 30 years has been taken in hand by the National Trust to ensure its long-term survival.

The north half of the island is leased to the Dorset Wildlife Trust. There are viewing hides to allow visitors to watch the important populations of birds on the lagoon. For part of the season visitors can follow a self-guided nature trail. At other times, guided tours are organised.

An oak tree on the island's central plateau

A nineteenth-century lithograph showing the Villa and the area of St Andrew's Bay reclaimed by Col Waugh in the 1850s as pasture-land. (It now forms part of the lagoon)

One of the two freshwater lakes in the centre of the island

The Brownsea woodlands provide a rich habitat for a wide range of birds and animals, including Tawny Owls and Woodcock

Wildlife

About 200 red squirrels live on Brownsea Island. They are a rare sight in mainland Britain, where they have been driven out by their larger and more successful grey cousin. The island's mature pinewoods provide red squirrels with an ideal habitat and source of food. These shy animals are easiest to see in the morning, when they are at their most active, and in the autumn, when they are most numerous.

In 1896 Kenneth Balfour introduced the Japanese Sika deer to Brownsea, where they flourished until the 1934 fire drove them from the island. In recent years they have begun to swim back across Poole harbour. Their return has been a mixed blessing. Sika deer are undoubtedly a decorative and historically important addition to the island's wildlife, but they are as destructive as rabbits. They prevent young saplings from naturally regenerating, and strip the bark from sallow and sweet chestnuts. Like the red squirrels, they tend to avoid man, browsing in the dense undergrowth of the central woodlands and marsh.

Brownsea attracts many other animals as well. At least 24 species of dragonfly have been recorded on the island, which also supports important populations of butterflies and bats.

A Sika deer

One of Brownsea's red squirrels – an increasingly rare sight on the mainland

The Lagoon

Two views of the lagoon

Until the 1930s the pasture-land reclaimed from St Andrew's Bay was kept drained by a windmill. Mrs Bonham-Christie allowed the area to be inundated once again, but the enclosing sea-wall survived, so that the area became a non-tidal lagoon of brackish water, mud-flat and reeds - a habitat which is now extremely rare on the south coast.

During the winter many species of wader, including the picturesque Avocet, congregate here, when their normal feeding grounds around Poole harbour are covered at high tide. In the spring Common and Sandwich Terns fly in from Africa to breed on the shore of the lagoon. Other migrant birds use it as a convenient resting-place on their long spring journey north to nesting sites in Scandinavia and Russia. The autumn brings flocks of them returning south for the winter. Shelduck are a common sight all the year round and breed on the island in considerable numbers. The Little Egret nested here for the first time in Britain and there is also a large heronry on the island.

This part of the island is managed by the Dorset Wildlife Trust. There are viewing hides around the lagoon, including the Public Hide, open to all visitors.

A Shelduck on the lagoon

Brownsea today and in the future

Looking after a special place like Brownsea Island is a balancing act. The National Trust aims to not only conserve natural habitats and historic buildings, but also provide access for people to visit, enjoy and learn about the island. The Trust also needs to generate sufficient income to pay for its work.

In summer, the Brownsea Open Air Theatre provides an opportunity for visitors to enjoy evening performances of Shakespeare and raise funds for the work of the Trust. These events and various learning programmes help visitors, including thousands of young people, to appreciate and learn about Brownsea. The Outdoor Activity Centre allows young people from all over the world to enjoy this special place through camping, lodge accomodation, sailing, archery and other outdoor pursuits.

One of the biggest tasks is to remove the rhododendron and other invasive species to allow woodland and heath to regrow. This is key to the survival of the red squirrel population. As with much of the Trust's work this could not be done without the help of hundreds of volunteers. One of the long-term issues for the National Trust is that of coastal erosion and rising sea levels. As with other management issues, decisions wil be made with the advice of experts and stakeholders.

Much has already been done with your support, but the Trust still needs your help as a visitor, member, volunteer or donor to ensure the long-term future of Brownsea Island, which gives so much pleasure to so many.

The shoreline on the south-east coast of the island

The quayside buildings on the east coast with the Dorset mainland in the background

The sandy beaches of the Studland peninsula lie to the south of Brownsea. Beyond are the chalk cliffs of Old Harry